The Power to Overcome Fear

Breaking Free From the Enemy's Grip!

Thedoshia L. Shealey

DivineCrossingx, Inc.
Psalms 37:23
creative design solutions

DivineCrossingx Publishing Company

DivineCrossingx Publishing Books
Published by DivineCrossingx Publishing Company
Publishers Since 2007

Printed and bound in the United States of America.

DivineCrossingx Publishing Company
P.O.Box 652
Austell, Georgia 30168

Shealey L. Thedoshia
The Power to Overcome Fear / Thedoshia L. Shealey.
p. cm.
ISBN 978-0-9793217-1- 9

1. Spiritual – Motivational. 2. Non-Fiction. 3. Warner Robins (Georgia) – Non-Fiction. I. Title.

This body of work is a personal story and testimony of her struggle with fear and how she overcame it. The author has made every effort to provide accurate telephone numbers, source citations, and Internet addresses at the time of publication. Neither the publisher nor the author assumes any responsibility for errors, or for changes that occur after publication. Furthermore, the publisher does not have any control over and does not assume any responsibility for author or third-party websites or their content.

Table of Contents

ঙ Dedication ঙ

Aunt Janie M. Green

This book is dedicated to the memory of my Great Aunt
Janie M. Green. A remarkable woman of God, Janie was
known throughout the community as an *encourager*. Full of
wisdom, she always remained ready and willing to share
her faith with those who she came in contact with.

 Encouraging others to pursue their dreams, Janie
enthusiastically advised all to acknowledge God in
everything that they set out to do.

Her continuous prayers and support throughout the years
has helped pave the way for many.

An awesome mentor and woman of God, Janie's life
exemplified that of a true and humble servant.

I cannot thank God enough for allowing me the privilege to
be part of your life here on earth.
Janie, you are greatly missed…

◌ Acknowledgements ◌

To my Savior and Lord Jesus Christ: Thank you for your awesome gift and for entrusting me to share the message of this book. Without you I could not have experienced my breakthrough! Father, thank you for the gifts you have invested in me, I give you all the praise, glory, and honor! Thank you to my wonderful husband Louis. Your encouragement and support has meant so much to me. Thank you for believing in me, for giving me that extra nudge and holding me accountable when I needed it. I love you and am forever grateful to God for bringing us together.

Special thanks to Theodore R. Allen III, author of *The Steps of a Good Man… Discovering Your Path to Successful Living,* for his support and added expertise. Theo, thank you so much for encouraging me to embark on the journey of writing this book. And thanks for giving me that extra push when I needed it. To DivineCrossingx Publishing Company, thank you for your willingness to invest your time and expertise to edit and review this book. It has been made all the more better because of you.

Pastor Gregory & Geraldine McClendon: Thank you so much for the solid teachings and guidance you have imparted in my family. Thank you for the many prayers you have prayed and the solid covering you bestowed upon my family throughout the years. You have been the epitome of what God called and ordained for a true Pastor/Shepherd to be. Your labor in the Lord is not unnoticed neither is it in vain. May God continue to richly bless you!

Bishop Jeff & Lisa Poole, Thank you for your continuous labor in the Lord. Thank you for rightly dividing the Word of Truth and making it readily available to your flock. May God continue to richly bless you as He enlarges your territory for the KINGDOM!

Thedoshia

ଔ A Prayer for the Journey ଔ

Dear Reader,

As you prepare to take your journey through this book, my prayer is that you are sensitive to the Spirit of God so that you may receive revelation knowledge from the Word of God.

Thedoshia

Introduction

It affects people of all ages and it does not discriminate against race, religion, or social class. Its ultimate goal is to deter you from reaching your true potential and God given giftedness. Moreover, it is designed to prevent you from becoming the person you were created to be, and hinder you from experiencing the life God has ordained for you. What is it? What is this backdoor debilitating disease that seeks to rob you of your very existence? What is this vacillating widget that wants to infiltrate every aspect of life and destroy you to the core? This destructive agent that is out to paralyze you is known as *F.E.A.R.* or

False Evidence Appearing Real

Are you someone who is living with fear? Do you find yourself crippled by the effects of fear? Is it your desire to live fear free? Although there are many in the body of Christ who have laid down their arms against fear, this is not the will of God for the believer. God would have us to stand our ground and overcome fear through our faith, partnered with revelation from His Word. Whatever your life and external environment may consist of, if you are a child of God, you can take authority over and conquer the fear in your life. Having experienced struggles of my own, please allow me to reassure those of you who are dealing with this issue. There is absolutely nothing to be ashamed of. In fact, there are probably people, most likely within your own circles, who like you, are secretly battling fear in some area of their lives. Some of whom may be so crippled by its effects that it has become part of their normality. Although the enemy would attempt to deceive you into believing that fear is not an issue in your life, God already knows what you are dealing with and to what extent. It is his desire that you come into the knowledge of **His Truth** and receive your deliverance. In order to receive a true deliverance, we must be willing to become transparent. It is vital that you be completely open and honest, not only with God but with yourself. In this way, you will experience a true move of God as He ushers you into a new level in your walk with him. Too long has the enemy held believers captive and bound with fear. It's time that we take authority over fear; build ourselves and one another up as we move into our divine callings and Gods' ordained destiny for our lives. Proverbs 4:7 says, "Wisdom is the principal thing, and with all your getting get understanding." In other words, wisdom is the primary or the main thing and in all that we obtain we should gain understanding. In all of our attaining, we are told to acquire understanding, but it doesn't stop there. We are expected to **apply** the understanding we receive to our lives. Wisdom can be defined as knowledge that is rightly applied. How can we properly apply something to our lives without possessing the proper knowledge? Hosea 4:6 says, "My people are destroyed for lack of knowledge." To be effective in the Kingdom, we must have both adequate and proper knowledge. Therefore, it is crucial that we not only **gain understanding** about fear, but also **apply** what we learn to our lives on a daily basis.

I have come in contact with many individuals, who are dealing with fear, and in my experience, I have found that while most people do realize they have a fear issue, many are unaware of how to break free from its' grip. Plagued with fear as a child and on into adulthood, I became disillusioned at the thought of contending with the enemy each time I set forth to engage in ministry. After becoming annoyed with the attacks, I began to identify them for what they were and set out to take authority over it. Determined to no longer allow the enemy to maintain an advantage over me, I began earnestly seeking deliverance in this area.

While diligently seeking God, and with much prayer, I received deliverance by applying the wisdom contained within the Word of God to my life on a daily basis. The contents of this book are a result of the revelations I have received from God in my quest for deliverance. This is a result of what I have walked through in my own personal life experience. Because God is no respecter of persons, you too can be delivered and empowered as you progress toward your destiny and God's higher call for your life.

The Layout of this Book

This book is broken up into several chapters. We will begin by taking an in depth look at the definition of fear. After we have reviewed various definitions, we will discuss the origin and purpose of fear. In Chapter Two, we explore several ways in which fear affects us as individuals. This chapter will allow you to gain a solid understanding of the effects of fear in your life. Chapter Three covers the power, love, and sound mind that God has given to us as believers. In Chapter Four we discuss basic steps which **must** be taken as you prepare to take authority over this area of your life. The steps in this section are not limited to this particular subject matter, but should be utilized consistently in all areas of our lives. In Chapter Five we will discuss ways to ambush the enemy as we go into battle. I will share actions which you are **required** to take on your journey to deliverance. Chapter Six will cover the issue of love. Finally, in Chapter Seven we will deal solely with maintaining your deliverance. Here you will learn the importance and necessities of preserving this area of your life. The end of each chapter is followed by a short prayer. Please feel free to use them on your journey to destroying and overcoming the power of the enemy in this area of your life. These prayers are scriptural and if you speak them, **in faith**, over your life they will not only build your spirit man, but according to the Word of God, will dispatch the Angels of the Most High on your behalf. If you grasp hold of these truths, you are guaranteed to see results!

Are you annoyed and fed up with the attacks you have encountered? Are you ready to claim the victory in this area of your life? Then come, let us take a walk through the Word of God, so that you too may gain the necessary understanding to conquer and annihilate this thing called fear, according to Gods' wisdom and revelation from His Word. Let us pray.

PRAYER

Father, I come boldly to the throne of grace asking, (believing I have received) for a greater level of understanding concerning fear. As I incline my ears to hear your voice I ask the Holy Spirit to illuminate the scriptures and guide me in applying what I learn to my life. God grant me divine revelation concerning fear and give me wisdom as I seek to demolish its power in my life. Fill me with the knowledge of your will in all wisdom and spiritual understanding. Strengthen me as I commit to taking the necessary steps, in partnership with you, to ensure my complete and total deliverance from fear.

In Jesus' Name I Pray
Amen

CHAPTER 1
Fear Defined

We have a tendency to think of fear from a carnal state of mind, viewing it only as an emotion. In this context, fear is a natural human response that we all experience; however, throughout this book we will take a look at fear from a spiritual perspective. As I began to research the definition of fear, I found that it can be defined as any or all of the following: "A spirit, an emotion of negative feeling, a weapon, and a stronghold." Let us pause to take a closer look at these definitions.

Fear as a Spirit

The word of God clearly identifies fear as a spirit:

"For God hath not given us the _spirit_ of fear; but of power, and of love, and of a sound mind."

2 Timothy 1:7 (KJV)

A spirit is defined as a supernatural or unseen being that can become visible or audible to humans.

1

"We are not wrestling against flesh and blood, but against principalities, against powers, against the rulers of the darkness of this world, and against spiritual wickedness in high places."

Ephesians 6:12

In other words, Paul explains that we are not fighting against human beings, but against spiritual beings, against spiritual forces and authorities who are rulers of darkness and who possess power in the spirit realm. In this context, a fear spirit is sent on assignment to invade our lives, ultimately seeking to attach itself to the core of our beings, in an effort to hinder us from pursuing and living out the will God for our lives.

Fear as an Emotion

"For God hath not given us the spirit of _fear_; but of power, and of love, and of a sound mind."

2 Timothy 1:7 (KJV)

As previously stated, fear, as an emotional reaction, is part of our normal human response. According to Webster's Dictionary, fear is defined as: A feeling of alarm or disquiet caused by an **awareness** and **expectation** of danger. An emotion one experiences in the presence of danger, whether **real** or **perceived**. It is the act of living in a state **fearful**

anticipation. As sons and daughters of the Most High God, we must understand that this type of fear is not meant to be part of our normality.

From this perspective, the power of suggestion is used to induce a sense of anxiety into our lives. Its ultimate goal is to manipulate us into adopting a fearful mentality, causing us to live with a fearful anticipation, expecting danger to come upon us in one form or another.

Fear as a Weapon

"But no <u>weapon</u> that is formed against you shall prosper, and every tongue that shall rise against you in judgment you shall show to be in the wrong."

Isaiah 54:17 (AMP)

A weapon is an instrument or device used to attack another; a tool used to intimidate, overcome (conquer), persuade, or get an advantage of someone. It is a tool which is used to apply force on another for the purpose of causing harm or damage. It extends to include anything used to gain an advantage over another. Fear, in this context is an instrument which has been crafted as an intimidation device. It is used to gain an advantage over us as believers.

Fear as a Stronghold

For the weapons of our warfare are not physical [weapons of flesh and blood], but they are mighty before God for the overthrowing and destruction of <u>strongholds</u>.

2 Corinthians 10:4 (AMP)

A **stronghold** is defined as a heavily fortified defensive structure. It is an area that is strengthened and secured usually militarily; A fortress. A stronghold is meant to be a place of refuge, but can become a place of confinement. In this context, a stronghold is a specific area of our lives in which the enemy has succeeded in establishing a foothold. It is a place where he seeks to hold us captive, restricting our ability to freely function. The Greek word for fear is *Deilia,* meaning timidity or cowardice. Digging deeper I discovered that *Deilia* comes from *Deilos* which means fearful, timid, and faithless. Further study revealed that *Deilos* was derived from the root word *Deos* meaning dread which implies great fear. Extracting from the previous definitions, we can confidently say that fear is a cowardice and faithless spirit that is employed as a weapon, with the intent of causing us to anticipate danger. It provides a channel through which the dispatcher is able to gain an advantage over the intended victim, ultimately seeking to establish a place of confinement and restriction.

If the scriptures clearly reveal that God did not impart this type of spirit into us, the question remains, where then does fear originate?

The Origin and Purpose of Fear

According to Word, this type of fear does not come from God. God cannot impart a spirit of cowardice or faithlessness to us because these things are against His very nature. Furthermore, he has given us freewill and would never seek to manipulate his children in an attempt to gain an advantage over us, whether by confinement, restriction, or any other means. Paul warns us to, **"be sober, vigilant, because our adversary the devil, <u>as</u> a roaring lion, walks about seeking whom he may devour." (1 Peter 5:8-KJV).** Notice one key word (as). When lions hunt, one tactic they use is a fear tactic. After creeping up on its prey, a lion lets out a roar so ferocious that it literally causes paralysis. Once paralyzed with fear, the unsuspecting prey is overtaken, falling victim to its attacker.

The enemy operates in a similar way, imitating the strategy of a lion; he creeps into our lives, often undetected, and injects a spirit of fear which causes paralysis, as we are often are too intimidated to move in any direction. Likewise, just as a lion's prey, if we are not careful we too will fall victim to the enemy's tactic. When we come to this understanding and realize the enemy's bluff, we can call him out with the Word of God and he has no choice but to "tuck his tail and run."

PRAYER

Father, I thank you for granting me a greater understanding of fear. I realize that fear does not come from you and truly believe it to be your desire that I live free of fear. I take authority over fear and cast down vain imaginations and every high thing that lifts itself against the knowledge of God. I bring my thoughts captive into obedience to Christ. I loose my mind from old patterns of thinking, and I bind my mind to the mind of Christ. I have the mind of Christ and I meditate on things that are true, honest, just, pure, lovely, and of good report. I decree and declare that fear has no place in my life. I bind the stronghold of fear and declare that its works, fruit, and links are dead in my life. I loose you from your assignment against me and command you to go forth into outer darkness and remain there. I seal this prayer in the power of the Holy Spirit and by the blood of Jesus.

In Jesus' Name I Pray
Amen

❧ REFLECTIONS ❧

❧ REFLECTIONS ❧

CHAPTER 2

Understanding the Effects of Fear & How the Enemy Operates

Access Granted: Negative Manifestations

The book of Job is a revealing book. Not only does it provide us with an excellent illustration of how the enemy gains access into our lives, it also gives us good insight into how we as believers provide opportunities for the enemy to attack us by granting him the right of passage into our lives. As we seek to better understand this issue, let us take a closer look at the revealing story of Job's life.

⁶ "Now there was a day when the sons (the angels) of God came to present themselves before the Lord, and Satan (the adversary and accuser) also came among them."

⁷ "And the Lord said to Satan, from where did you come? Then Satan answered the Lord, from going to and fro on the earth and from walking up and down on it."

⁸ "And the Lord said to Satan, have you considered My servant Job, that there is none like him on the earth, a blameless and upright man, one who [reverently] fears God and abstains from and shuns evil [because it is wrong]?"

⁹ "Then Satan answered the Lord, Does Job [reverently] fear God for nothing?"

¹⁰ "Have You not put a hedge about him and his house and all that he has, on every side? You have conferred prosperity and happiness upon him in the work of his hands, and his possessions have increased in the land."

¹¹ "But put forth Your hand now and touch all that he has and he will curse You to Your face."

¹² "And the Lord said to Satan (the adversary and the accuser), Behold, all that he has is in your power, only upon the man himself put not forth your hand. So Satan went forth from the presence of the Lord."

Job 1:6-12 (AMP)

There is so much to learn in these scriptures. When I initially read this passage for revelation I was blown away, and I think you will be too. Lets us take a moment to examine these scriptures more closely so that we can gain the necessary understanding to effectively deal with fear. First, verse six tells us that the sons of God (the angels) came to present themselves before the Lord and Satan also came among them. This scripture clearly illustrates Satan's ability to travel between the heaven and earth realms. Notice God's question to Satan in verse seven and his response. Intent on wreaking havoc in the earth, Satan, the god of this world, walks throughout the earth patrolling it seeking anyone he can manipulate. His sole purpose is to steal, kill, and destroy.

This is why we are commanded in 1 Peter 5:8 to,

"Be sober, vigilant, because our adversary the devil, as a roaring lion, walks about seeking whom he may devour."
1 Peter 5:8 (KJV)

Although Satan is not all knowing, he can and does sense fear. Because fear is his belief system, he operates through it. Satan, having sensed Job's fear, saw the perfect opportunity to launch an attack on this man of God. I believe that he had already considered Job as a potential subject, but recognized that God had a hedge of protection around Job. I further believe that Satan sought to gain clarity as to the extent to which he could afflict Job. This passage of scripture provides us with awesome revelation and gives us a clear understanding as to how limited the enemy really is. He too has to report to the Creator and Author of the universe to give an account of his activities here in the earth. God has Satan on a leash. As Christians who are in right standing with God, this should bring us great comfort. The enemy has to first gain permission to test us and can only afflict us to the extent in which God allows him to. And even in the midst of our tests and trials we have the added reassurance of Roman 8:28.

After Satan responds, God poses yet another question.

> [8] "And the Lord said to Satan, have you considered My servant Job, that there is none like him on the earth, a blameless and upright man, one who [reverently] fears God and abstains from and shuns evil [because it is wrong]?"

Job 1:8 (AMP)

Notice how He gets straight to the point. It almost seems as if God began speaking before Satan could finish. In His sovereignty, God already knew the intent of Satan's heart in testing Job. He knew Satan had already considered Job.

> [9] "Then Satan answered the Lord, Does Job [reverently] fear God for nothing? [10]Have You not put a hedge about him and his house and all that he has, on every side? You have conferred prosperity and happiness upon him in the work of his hands, and his possessions have increased in the land. [11]But put forth Your hand now and touch all that he has and he will curse You to Your face."

Job 1:9-11 (AMP)

The enemy recognizes authority and knows he is required to submit and obey. Verse ten clearly illustrates this fact. Satan recognizes God's protective hand in the lives of believers. Following Satan's acknowledgement of God's provision and protection over Job's life, he scoffs God, suggesting that Job's devotion was contingent on His blessings in his life (Job 1:10). He then makes a blunt statement saying, "But now put forth your hand and touch all that he has, and he will curse you to your face."

Now, notice God's response to Satan:

> [12] "**And the Lord said to Satan (the adversary and the accuser), Behold, all that he has is in your power, only upon the man himself put not forth your hand. So Satan went forth from the presence of the Lord."**

> **Job 1:12 (AMP)**

Having received permission and clarity, Satan leaves the presence of God and proceeds to afflict Job by destroying his possessions (Job 1:10-12). During the attack on Job the enemy destroyed all of Job's possessions. And after losing everything he had, including his sons and daughters, Job demonstrated intense grief according to the custom of his day. He then acknowledged God's sovereignty and began to worship (Job 1:20). I believe Job's fearful mentality opened a door for the enemy to gain access into his life. It is my belief that Satan knew he had a right to access Job's life, and appeared before God to gain permission and clearance as to the extent to which he could afflict this man of God. As Christians, this should bring us consolation. Satan dares not touch the child of God before consulting with God, even when we grant him access into our lives because of our lack of knowledge or disobedience. We can have confidence knowing that even in the midst of our trials the test has been predetermined and measured by God. The enemy can only test us to the extent to which God allows him. And we have the added assurance that God will cause all things to work out for our benefit. Although Job knew God was in control of his life. His statement in chapter three clearly indicates that he had acquired a fearful expectation of something harmful coming upon him. And because he continued to harbor that mentality, the enemy sought to afflict him to an even greater degree. This can be seen in Job 2:1-5. Once again after appearing before God and obtaining clarity, Satan sets out to attack Job yet again, but this time to a greater degree. And with one condition set before him (the sparing of Job's life), Satan launches a relentless attack against Job's body. (Job 2:1-7)

Job was a man described by God as being blameless and upright, one who reverenced God, and avoided evil (Job 1:8, 2:3). During that time Job was known to be the wealthiest man in the region, because God had caused everything he touched to prosper, so much so that it overflowed throughout his household and onto all he possessed. Not only did God bless the work of Job's hands, but He had also placed a hedge of protection around Job and all that he owned. Job had no lack…he had all he could every need and more (Job 1:3, 10). Yet despite all the prosperity and protection he had, Job harbored a secret that was rooted so deeply, that perhaps no one close to him ever realized. What was this secret?

> **"For the thing which I _greatly feared_ is come upon me, and _that which I dreaded_ has happened to me."**
> **Job 3:25 (KJV)**

Job may or may not have verbalized his fears prior to his attacks; there is no mention of this in the scriptures, yet according to his own words in Job 3:25, it existed. Although he may not have given voice to his fears, the thoughts were there and to some extent he meditated on them. A fearful mindset not only gave the enemy access into Job's life, but provided a channel through which negative manifestations could occur. I believe Satan, having sensed Job's fear, appeared before God in both instances, to gain clarity as to the extent to which he could afflict Job. Notice in chapter 2, the second attack was more severe than the first. This perhaps, was due to Job's continued fearful mentality. It is important to understand that just as there are degrees of faith, there are also degrees of attacks resulting from possessing a fearful mentality. Because demonic spirits sense and operate through fear, when we operate in fear and outside of the measure of faith God has given us, we essentially become magnets for fear spirits. Granting them access and providing a means through which negative manifestations can occur in our lives. The level of fear we operate in determines the extent of access the enemy gains into our lives. The greater the degree of fear, the more severe the attacks and the more determined the enemy becomes to establish a stronghold in our lies and hinder our progress.

In contrast, God operates through faith, requiring us to exercise the measure of faith He has given us. In doing so we strengthen and build our faith muscles to a point where we begin to trust God in greater levels. This is essential as we advance from one level of glory to another. Hebrews 11:6 reminds us that it is impossible to please God without faith. Because faith is God's belief system, it both pleases and attracts him when we operate in it. The greater the degree of faith, the more attractive we become to God and the more excited and determined He becomes to meet our faith. I want you to get another revelation of this scripture, so let us look at Job 3:25 once again:

"For the thing which I _greatly feared_ is come upon me, and that which I _dreaded_ has happened to me."
Job 3:25 (KJV)

I'd like to place emphasis on this scripture. Because the opposite of fear is faith, a good faith confession would sound something like: That for which I have great faith for is coming upon me, and that for which I have confidence for is happening to me! Just a little something to think about…life and death truly are in the power of the tongue. We are commanded to give no place to the devil (Ephesians 4:27). Therefore, it is vital that we endeavor to secure all potential access points the enemy may seek to use as an entry point into our lives.

A Cluttered Spirit

²⁴ "Another parable He set forth before them, saying, the kingdom of heaven is like a man who sowed good seed in his field. ²⁵ But while he was sleeping, his enemy came and sowed also darnel (weeds resembling wheat) among the wheat, and went on his way. ²⁶ So when the plants sprouted and formed grain, the darnel (weeds) appeared also."

Matthew 13:24-26 (AMP)

Jesus shares an important truth in the parable of the tares. Upon closely examining this verse, this is the revelation I've received concerning it:

- ❖ Sowing = Hearing
- ❖ The Good Seed = The Word of God
- ❖ The Field = Our spirits
- ❖ The Enemy = Satan
- ❖ Darnel/Weeds = Doubt, Confusion, Fear
- ❖ Wheat = Our Harvest

When the Word of God is sown into our lives, we hear and receive it in our spirits. While we are distracted by the cares of life, the enemy, very cunningly sets out to infect the fruit of the harvest God desires to give us. He accomplishes this by sowing doubt, confusion, and fear amid our harvest. Fear causes spiritual miscarriages and abortions. Our spirits are receptacles for God's Word seed, and if we are not careful to guard against it, fear will cause us to forfeit the Word of God in our lives. We cannot hear from God or retain his seed if our spirits are cluttered. It is vital that we maintain a clear channel of communication if we are to clearly hear from God. How do we accomplish this?

"Be well balanced (temperate, sober of mind), be vigilant and cautious at all times; for that enemy of yours, the devil, roams around like a lion roaring [in fierce hunger], seeking someone to seize upon and devour."

1 Peter 5:8 (AMP)

Another translation reads:

"Be careful – watch out for the attacks from Satan, your great enemy. He prowls around like a hungry, roaring lion, looking for some victim to tear apart."

1 Peter 5:8 (TLB)

If we are to clearly hear from our great commissioner, we must maintain spirits that are clear and clutter free. We must be mindful to watch and pray.

Hindered Growth

"Do not neglect the gift that is in you, which was given to you by prophecy, with the laying on of the hands of the elders."

1 Timothy 4:14 (NKJV)

Fear can have a debilitating effect in the lives of believers. Has God ever given you a specific task to accomplish and you knew without a doubt that it was in fact God directing you to do so? Did you immediately set out to accomplish it or did you wait and question God, as to whether or not He made the right decision in choosing you? Perhaps you questioned your ability to accomplish the task. If you are like me, and I trust that many of you are, you can probably say yes to the above statements. In fact, I think it's safe to say that many of us have, at some point in our lives during our walk with God, have run the other way when presented with a task that we perceived to be too big or unqualified to accomplish.

I recall one particular memory during childhood; my siblings and I were reared in church. My grandmother had given consent for us to become part of the children's choir. Always possessing a love for music and singing, I was thrilled. It was at the Harris Street Church of God that I initially began to publicly use my voice in this capacity. As time progressed, I was asked to lead a song. Never having being one to volunteer in the past, I somehow knew deep down the day would eventually arrive. After several rehearsals the day quickly approached when we would share with the church congregation. When the day arrived, I mysteriously woke up feeling sick…too sick to attend church that day. Already having plotted the situation out, I sent word by one of my sisters to inform the choir directors that I was not feeling well and would not be able to attend church that day. As the time neared when everyone would return from services that day, I waited anxiously to hear, how things turned out. To my delight…it worked. The day had come and passed. And I had successfully hidden the fact that I was scared stiff at the thought of singing in front of all those people. No one knew at the time, in fact they will probably find out after reading this book, just how terrified I was.

I often reminisce about the little girl who did not understand the power fear had over her life, nor the effects she would continue to wrestle with into her adulthood. For years I neglected a gift that God, through his Spirit had imparted in me. I had allowed fear to hinder me from using it. And for many years thereafter, it failed to grow or properly develop. This is why the Apostle Paul warns us not to neglect the gift of God that is in us, but instead to stir it up, or cultivate it. Neglect in the spiritual is as neglect in natural…they both lead to malnourishment. When we fail to cultivate our gifts it robs us of the ability to develop and mature in those areas. Oftentimes this causes us to become spiritually stagnant. We must come to an understanding that this is not the will of God. He desires that our gifts properly develop as we grow to a place of spiritual maturity in Him. How can we expect to be effective for the Kingdom if we fail to develop the specific areas of giftedness God has so graciously given us? All too often, we face the challenges of fear, perceiving them as obstacles instead of opportunities to glorify God. It wasn't until I became serious and determined to walk in my anointing that the tables turned. Exercising what God has placed in me has enabled me to not only develop but mature in it and more importantly, it edifies the body of believers and glorifies God. This is God's will for the Body of Christ.

Corroded Faith

"But without faith it is impossible to please Him, for he who comes to God must believe that he is, and that He is a rewarder of those who diligently seek Him."

Hebrews 11:6 (KJV)

Recall in the previous chapter, one of the Greek definitions for fear was faithless. Fear produces a doubtful heart and slowly eats away at our faith. Sadly enough, it also blocks our sense of God's presence in our lives. Fear is the opposite of faith and has no place in the life of a believer. Yet there are many Christians who operate in fear rather than faith. And as a result of fear, many cannot sense the presence of God in their lives and are living day to day with a sense of defeat. When we cannot sense the presence of God in our lives, we tend to become disconnected and will often begin viewing ourselves as victims rather than victors. The foundation of faith is that we must believe. It is mandatory for all who approach God. And according to the previous verse, God rewards us when we diligently seek Him in faith. Faith is our connection to the Father and we must work to develop and maintain it.

PRAYER

Father, thank you for your Word and the authority you have
given me in Christ Jesus. I come pleading the precious
blood of your son Jesus over and against the spirit of fear
and all its effects. You have given me authority over all the
power of the enemy. And I refuse to be cluttered, hindered,
or overwhelmed by fear. I bind the power of negative
manifestations in my life and in the lives of those with
whom I come in contact with. I bind the power of negative
words spoken to me and by me. I declare and decree that
they will not take root. Father, I ask you to release the
untapped power of the Holy Spirit in me. And when the
enemy comes against me I ask the Holy Spirit to lift up a
standard against him. As I release my faith into the
atmosphere I declare that I am free from the bondage of
fear.

In Jesus' Name I Pray
Amen

❧ REFLECTIONS ❧

○3 REFLECTIONS ○3

CHAPTER 3

Power, Love, and a Sound Mind

"For God did not give us the spirit of fear, but of power, and of love, and of a sound mind."

2 Timothy 1:7 (KJV)

Now that we have a better understanding of fear and its origin, let us examine the subject matter surrounding the power, love and sound mind that Paul explains we have received from God.

The Power of the Spirit

But ye shall receive _power_, after that the Holy Ghost has come upon you: and ye shall be witnesses unto me both in Jerusalem, and in Judea, and in Samaria, and unto the uttermost part of the earth.

Acts 1:8 (KJV)

God, through his Holy Spirit has imparted in us the spirit of power, of love, and of a sound mind. At the moment we accepted Jesus as our Savior, God the Holy Spirit indwelt us and sealed us as his own. When we received his indwelling, we also received his power. Likewise, as we continue and mature in our Christian walk, we receive the infilling of the Holy Spirit. This infilling occurs at crucial moments throughout our growth process. It is during these moments that we are refreshed with a new burst of his power to accomplish the Fathers' work. That power is dunamis, dynamite in its working. Ephesians 3:20 explains,

"God is able to do exceeding abundantly above all that we ask or think, according to the _power_ that works within us."

Paul further expressed this concept in his letter to the Colossians, stating:

"Wherefore I also labour, striving according to his working, which _worketh in me mightily_."

Colossians 1:29 (KJV)

The Amplified reads, "For this I labor [unto weariness], striving with all the superhuman energy which He [God] so mightily enkindles and works within me."

Paul makes reference to the supernatural power of God at

work within him as the channel through which he is able to do the work of the ministry God has called him to do. The Spirit of God has imparted that same power in us. As sons and daughters of the Most High God, it is vital that we acknowledge, understand, and utilize the power of God that is in each of us. We must grasp hold of the knowledge of what Jesus' death, burial, and resurrection accomplished for us. He did not die for believers to live fearful lives, but he came that we might have life and have it more abundantly – in the fullest measure (John 10:10). Part of that abundant life is rooted in our obtaining the proper knowledge of God's manifest power within us, tapping into it, and using it to accomplish God's will in the earth.

The Love of the Spirit

[17] That Christ may dwell in your hearts by faith; that ye being rooted and grounded *in love*, [18] may be able to comprehend with all saints what is the breadth, and the length, and the depth, and the height; [19] And to know the love of Christ, which passeth knowledge, that ye might be filled with all the fullness of God.

Ephesians 3:17-19 (KJV)

In this passage of scripture, Paul expresses his desire for Christ to dwell in our hearts by faith, so that we being rooted and grounded in love may be able to comprehend the breadth, length, depth, and height of the love of God. He goes on to pray that we be filled with all the fullness of God. The question arises, how then are we filled with all the fullness of God? How is the love of God birthed in our hearts? I am glad you asked. The answer is found in the Word of God.

Scriptures clearly communicates that God is love:

Beloved, let us love one another: for love is of God; and every one that loveth is born of God, and knoweth God. He that loveth not knoweth not God; for God is love.

1 John 4:8 (KJV)

In the book of Romans Paul writes,

"Hope maketh not ashamed; because the love of God is shed abroad in our hearts by the Holy Ghost which is given unto us.

Romans 5:5 (KJV)

Another translation of this verse reads,

"We are able to hold our heads high no matter what happens and know that all is well, for we know how dearly God loves us, and we feel this warm love everywhere within us because God has given us the Holy Spirit to fill our hearts with his love."

Romans 5:5 (TLB)

God the Father, the Holy Spirit, and Jesus are one, they all coexist and work together to ensure that we come into an understanding of God's love for us. Each of them plays a part in this process. Here we see how this is accomplished.

- ❖ God expressed his love toward us while we were yet sinners by sending Christ, his only begotten son into the world to bear the sins of those who would accept him as their Savior (John 3:16; Rom.5:8).

- ❖ Jesus explained that he received a commandment from the Father, and willingly lay down his life for the sheep, those of us who would accept and follow him (John10:15-18). This was his initial expression of love toward us.

- ❖ Filling believers with the love of God is a work of the Holy Spirit. He has been commissioned by God to introduce and make real the love of God within us (Romans 5:5).

Each person of the Trinity undertook a specific responsibility, and actively engaged in fulfilling it. With that being said, we too have specific roles that we must fulfill, but we will discuss more of that in chapter six.

The Mind of the Spirit

The Apostle Paul poses a series of rhetorical question in Romans 11:34-35. It reads,

"For who can know the mind of the Lord? Who knows

enough to be his counselor or guide? And who could ever offer to the Lord enough to induce him to act?"

Romans 11:34 -35 (TLB)

Because God's ways and thoughts are higher than ours, in and of ourselves, we cannot possible know what is in the mind of God. The revelation of God we receive is granted us through the work of the Holy Spirit. Once again, because the persons of the Holy Trinity are one, the mind of God is both exclusive and inclusive to God the Father, God the Son, and God the Holy Spirit. Exclusive, because their minds are one and restricted from outside infiltration. Inclusive, because their mind is undivided and they have complete knowledge of one another. This is illustrated in the following verse:

"And God said, Let us make man in our image, after our likeness: **and let him have dominion over the fish of the sea, and the fowl of the air, and over the cattle, and over all the earth, and over every creeping thing that creepeth upon the earth."**

Genesis 1:26 (KJV)

All scripture, (the whole bible) was given to us by inspiration of God... it is God breathed (2 Timothy 3:16a).

Holy men of God spoke as they were moved by the Holy Spirit (1 Peter 1:21). John 1:1 reads, "In the beginning was the Word, and the Word was with God, and the Word was God. The Word was made flesh, and dwelt among us (John 1:14). Jesus came out from the presence of the Father and spoke the expressed will of God in the earth.

How then do we receive a sound mind? I'm glad you asked. We are admonished in Romans 12:2 to be transformed by the renewing of our minds. Our minds can only be renewed by the Word of God. As we study and meditate on God's Word, the Holy Spirit illuminates the scriptures to us. He speaks to us and in us what he hears of the Father. By allowing the Holy Spirit, in conjunction with the Word of God, to renew our minds we adopt a new mentality. The more Word we consume, the more the Holy Spirit works to maintain stable and durable mindsets within us. It is essentially a partnership…one that requires teamwork and equal participation. Are you doing your part?

PRAYER

Father, I come in the name of your resurrected son, Jesus the Christ, acknowledging that fear does not come from you. According to 2 Timothy 1:7, you have imparted in me a spirit of power, love, and a sound mind. I now give you total claim to my life and I pray that the power of the Holy Spirit will rise up in me and fill me with your love until it overflows. I take authority over fear and plead the blood of Jesus over my mind. I am being transformed by the renewing of my mind, and I declare that no weapon formed against me will prosper. I have the mind of Christ and I am filled with the knowledge of your will in all wisdom and spiritual understanding. I am the righteousness of God in Christ Jesus. You have raised me up together with Him and made us sit together in heavenly places. Thank you for blessing me with all spiritual blessings in Christ.

In Jesus' Name I Pray
Amen

ɛ REFLECTIONS ɛ

_____

_____

_____

_____

_____

_____

_____

_____

_____

_____

_____

_____

_____

_____

_____

_____

❧ REFLECTIONS ❧

CHAPTER 4
Preparing to Fight: A Spiritual Journey

"From the days of John the Baptist until now, the kingdom of heaven has been forcefully advancing, and forceful men lay hold of it."

Matthew 11:12 (NIV)

As sons and daughters of God, the enemy should be intimidated by us. When we are walking in authority, he is. Satan is well aware of our potential and the damage we are capable of causing him. This is why he fights so desperately to keep us bound. According to Matthew, the kingdom of heaven has been forcefully advancing, and those who use force take possession of it. The kingdom of heaven should be steadily advancing, however, there are many Christians who do not possess the proper knowledge of the authority they have in Christ Jesus. Many are waiting on God to move when He has already made the provision and given the commission. We must come to an understanding that God has already provided us with what we need to advance His Kingdom here in the earth. With that being said, we cannot simply sit back and wait on

God…He is waiting on us. Simply put, there are some things that require us to confront the enemy and take by force. However, before we can go into battle, there are requirements that we must meet if we are to be effective. What are they?

[11] "Put on all of God's armor so that you will be able to stand firm against all strategies of the devil. [12] For we are not fighting against flesh-and-blood enemies, but against evil rulers and authorities of the unseen world, against mighty powers in this dark world, and against evil spirits in the heavenly places." [13] "Therefore, put on every piece of God's armor so you will be able to resist the enemy in the time of evil. Then after the battle you will still be standing firm. [14] Stand your ground, putting on the belt of truth and the body armor of God's righteousness. [15] for shoes put on the peace that comes from the Good News so that you will be fully prepared. [16] In addition to all of these, hold up the shield of faith to stop the fiery arrows of the devil. [17] Put on salvation as your helmet, and take the sword of the Spirit, which is the word of God. [18] Pray in the Spirit at all times and on every occasion. Stay alert and be persistent in your prayers for all believers everywhere."

Ephesians 6:11-18 (NLT)

It is essential that we have on the whole armor of God, if we are going to be effective. The preceding scriptures tell us what they are and how we should use them. So let us examine them more closely.

Standing Your Ground

As a child, I recall witnessing a several fights between individuals. In many cases, a disagreement usually occurred between two individuals who were determined to maintain their stance in the situation. Oftentimes, the disagreement would start in one place and a fight would follow in another. Whatever the situation and setting, in any fight or battle, one is required to stand their ground or territory. If we are to effectively guard ourselves from the attacks of the enemy, we must be prepared to stand our ground. This means laying hold to the Truth of Gods' Word and attaching ourselves to it. It also signifies a "digging in the heels" so to speak. When we dig our heels in, we usually have our minds made up about a certain situation or thing, with a refusal to change our minds.

As Christians, we are commanded to stand our ground against the enemy. We are to embrace the Truth of God's Word about a situation, take a stance and dig our heels in. Proverbs 28:1 says, "the wicked flee when no man pursueth: but the righteous are bold as a lion." (KJV). We are the righteousness of God in Christ, and as sons and daughters of the Most High God; we are to have boldness in God, and in His ability to move on our behalves and work thru us. We are to have boldness rooted in the knowledge of who God has called us to be and what He has called us to do for the Kingdom. All too often, the enemy has Christians on the defense while he is steadily attacking and seemingly advancing his kingdom. That is not the position God intends for us to assume. The truth is that we should have the enemy on the defensive. We are to have a daring confidence to go into the enemy's camp and recover what he has stolen from us. We are to have the audacity to stand toe-to-toe against the enemy, stare him in his face and command him to submit to our authority. Why? Because we are Christ's and God has given us the authority to do so.

We must understand our positions as children of God. When we learn the truth of who we are in God, we will begin to better understand our authority in Him and walk it out. In doing so, we will advance God's Kingdom in the earth. We must get to a place where we stand our ground and resist the enemy with Truth. This is God's desire for the church. For further understanding, we will now take a few moments to discuss the parts of our armor. Each piece has a specific purpose. Let us examine them.

The Belt of Truth

The belt of truth is the part of the armor that holds other parts in their proper positions. Because God's Word is Truth, this signifies the fastening of God's Word around us. Another word for fastening is binding. In essence, when we put on the belt of truth we bind the Truth of God's Word to ourselves. An added advantage of the belt of truth is improved posture. There are certain types of belts which help to improve posture. One that comes to mind is a girdle. It is interesting to note that in some translations, the belt of truth is referred to as the girdle of truth. When properly applied the belt of truth improves our posture by compelling us to stand erect before both God and the enemy. As we stand upright before God we position ourselves to hear and receive of Him. And when we stand upright before the enemy we position ourselves to effectively exercise our authority through the spoken Word of God.

Without the Word of Truth, we are defenseless against the enemy's attacks and schemes. It is a vital component in our arsenal and must be utilized if we are to be effective in the Kingdom.

The Body Armor (Breastplate) of God's Righteousness

The body armor of God's righteousness is also known as the breastplate of righteousness. The breastplate serves to protect the upper torso of a soldier. When we are in right standing with God, the breastplate protects us from the accusations of the enemy. I believe the breastplate of righteousness refers to the moral character believers should possess. One way the enemy, also called the accuser of the brethren, seeks to infiltrate, infect, and alter the course of our lives is by constantly seeking out opportunities to accuse us before God and men. Can you imagine the dangers of engaging in a battle with the one referred to as "the father of lies while living a life of dishonesty? That is a guaranteed formula for disaster because when we fail to live lives of integrity and in obedience to God, we provide the enemy with access or an entry point into our lives. Maintaining Christ-like integrity is essential. Jesus became sin that we might be made the righteousness of God in him (2 Corinthians 5:21). We are the righteousness of God in Christ. And as Christians, we are called to be people of integrity. It is in Christ that we are made righteous unto God. And it is by abiding in Him that we maintain our right standing with God. As we abide in Christ, our breastplate is reinforced and the enemy's ability to penetrate it is diminished. Christ is our righteousness and it is through him that we are to portray God's righteousness in the earth.

Shoes of Peace

For shoes, we are told to put on the peace that comes from the Good News so that we will be fully prepared. The King James Version tells us to have our feet, "shod with the preparation of the gospel of peace." Shoes protect our feet, help us to stand properly, and enable us to move from one destination to another with greater ease. There is a peace that comes from the Word of God. It is the foundation upon which we must stand. The Word of God is the "good news" that we carry. Regardless of where life leads us, as Christians, we should always be prepared to impart a word of encouragement, empowerment, and peace. We are called to stand firmly upon the Word of God.

The Shield of Faith

Faith is to be used as a shield against the enemy's attacks. In 2 Corinthians 5:7, Paul tells us to "walk by faith and not by sight." (KJV). Walking in faith with total trust in God's Word, forms a shield around us and protects us from the fiery darts of the enemy, who will always throw seeds of doubt, discouragement, and confusion.

Our faith in God's Word is our shield of defense. With it we have the ability to extinguish the lies of the enemy. James 2:26 says, "As the body without the spirit is dead, so faith without works is dead." (KJV). Therefore, it is vital that we exercise faith in the Word of God. In doing so we consistently develop our faith and our shield becomes increasingly impenetrable by the attacks of the enemy.

The Helmet of Salvation

A soldiers' helmet protects his head. The head is considered to be one of the most vulnerable parts of the body. In 1 Thessalonians 5:8, the helmet of salvation is referred to as the hope of salvation.

But let us, who are of the day, be sober, putting on the breastplate of faith and love; and for a helmet, the hope of salvation.

1 Thessalonians 5:8 (KJV)

The New Living Translation reads:

But let us who live in the light be clearheaded, protected by the armor of faith and love, and wearing as our helmet the confidence of our salvation.

1 Thessalonians 5:8 (NLT)

The hope of salvation is the assurance we have in the promises of God's eternal Word. It is our confident expectation in God's ability to perform His Word.

The Sword of the Spirit

Ephesians 6:17 clearly identifies the Word of God as the sword of the Spirit. God used the voice of His word to speak creation into existence. As stated in Romans 4:17, it is He who calls things which are not as though they are. It was through the power of His Word that the universe was created. When He spoke things shifted into what He commanded them to be.

The Word of God is quick, and powerful, and sharper than any two-edged sword, piercing even to the dividing asunder of soul and spirit and of the joints and marrow, and is a discerner of thoughts and intents of the heart.

Hebrews 4:12 (KJV)

The Word of God, which is living and powerful, has been

made readily available to us as children of God. We are to take the Word of God and use it as both an offensive and defensive weapon against the enemy. However, we must understand that it is only when we **speak** the Word (Logos) of God that things will begin to shift and take shape in our lives, according to the will of God.

Pray in the Spirit

But you, beloved, build yourselves up [founded] on your most holy faith [make progress, rise like an edifice higher and higher], praying in the Holy Spirit.

Jude 20 (AMP)

We are commanded to pray in the Spirit as a means of building ourselves up spiritually. When we pray in the Spirit or allow the Spirit to pray through us, we tap into another realm of power, praying heavenly mysteries. Praying in the Spirit is a powerful means of communication. It allows us direct access to the very throne room of God and provides us with an advantage over the enemy, as he cannot understand what we are praying through the Spirit of God. These are all weapons God has provided to every believer (some offensive and some defensive) and before we engage in warfare we must ensure that we are properly suited with the whole armor of God.

PRAYER

Father, I realize that I am not wrestling against flesh and blood, but against powers, and principalities, against the rulers of darkness of this world, and against spiritual wickedness in high places. I thank you that the weapons of my warfare are not carnal but mighty through You [God] to the pulling down of strongholds, casting down imaginations and every high thing that lifts itself against the knowledge of God. I bring my thoughts captive and into obedience to Christ. According to Your Word in Ephesians 6, I put on the whole armor of God so that I am equipped to stand against the tactics and schemes of the enemy. Now I ask you to teach me how to apply the weapons You have provided for me so that I may wage an effective war against the enemy. Thank you for granting me understanding and insight.

In Jesus' Name I Pray
Amen

ℭ REFLECTIONS ℭ

❧ REFLECTIONS ❧

CHAPTER 5

Conquering Fear
Part 1: The Battle Begins

Take Action - Speak the Word of God

"So shall My Word be that goes forth out of my mouth: it shall not return to Me void [without producing any effect, useless], but it shall accomplish that which I please and purpose, and it shall prosper in the thing for which I sent it."

Isaiah 55:11 (AMP)

According to Isaiah 55:11 we have a divine promise that when we speak the written Word of God things will change. His Word will accomplish what it is sent to accomplish. However, we must declare it in faith believing that God is faithful to perform His Word being mindful that God is obligated by His Word and His Word alone.

Psalm 103:20 declares,

'Bless [affectionately, gratefully praise] the Lord, you His angels, you mighty ones who do His commandments, hearkening to the voice of His Word."

Psalm 103:20 (AMP)

The word hearken means to listen to attentively, or to give heed to. There is a host of angels attentively waiting for us to instruct them thru the Word of God. They are focused and alert, paying close attention to the words we speak. It is up to us as children of the Almighty to stand in the authority bestowed upon us and to give voice to the Word of God. In doing so, heavenly hosts of the Most High are dispatched to both move in our behalf and establish the will of the Father in the earth.

James 4:7 tells us to, "submit" ourselves to God, to resist the devil and he will flee from us. We submit to God by our obedience to His Word. And just as Jesus did when he was tempted in the garden (Matthew 4: 1-11), we effectively resist the devil by speaking the written Word of God. Remember, "Life and death are in the power of the tongue." God has made His Word available to us as a means of establishing His perfect Will in our lives and His Kingdom rule in the earth. As believers, we are His representatives here in the earth, we are His voice. And if we are to experience the fullness of God, be all He has called us to be and do, while at the same time establishing His kingdom reign in the earth, then speaking His Word must take precedence in our lives.

Take Action - Step Out in Faith

I recall a season in my life when fear hindered me from operating in my anointing. I would oftentimes become discouraged at the thought of even trying only to be overwhelmed with fear. Determined to embrace my deliverance, I made a conscious decision that no matter how bad the attack I was going to press through it. One incident which occurred many years ago comes to mind. I was asked to sing in a church program, and as the time neared, I became more uneasy than the day before. Somehow, I could sense that I was being faced with yet another attack. When the day finally arrived, I approached the front of the church and as I began to sing, it happened…the dreaded voice crack. Not only did my voice begin to tremble from nervousness and fear but to my utter surprise my legs literally began to shake beneath me. Determined to stand my ground, I refused to give in, remained standing, and confidently finished what I set out to do. You see, the Holy Spirit had enlightened me on a secret. He led me to James 2:26 which states "For as the body without the spirit is dead, so faith without works is dead also." (KJV). He revealed to me that one of the best ways to conquer the fear in my life was to take a stand and step out in faith despite how I felt. He made it clear to me that no matter how much faith I had to be delivered, if I never took a step towards receiving it, my faith availed nothing. It was as good as dead…faith without works is dead. The Holy Spirit then began to reassure me that regardless of what I was experiencing emotionally, He was right there with me, empowering me every step of the way. He revealed that stepping out in faith was a vital step in my journey to gain the victory in this area of my life.

One of the most powerful ways to overcome the fear in your life is to step out in faith and do it despite how you may be feeling. God operates through our faith not our feelings. When we make a conscious decision to trust God and take a leap of faith, He meets us where we are and begins to move in our behalf. Faith in action does something to receive what you believe God for. It places us in position to receive answers to our prayers. If you are unsure of what step God would have you to take, pray, and ask Him. He will surely reveal it to you, and when He does be willing to take the necessary step(s) toward receiving your deliverance. Remember, "Faith without works is dead." A faith step or action must accompany your faith! Now, let's move to another vital component…LOVE.

PRAYER

Father, thank You for the comfort of Your Word and knowing that You make all things work together for my good. I have total trust and confidence in Your Word and in Your ability to perform it. Thank you for the privilege and authority You have given me to utilize Your Word in my life. As I take authority over the spirit of fear, I declare that Your Word will not return void but will accomplish all I send it to accomplish according to Your Will. Thank you for the creative power of Your Word which causes Your perfect Will to be birth in my life. As I press forward, in faith, guide me along the paths you have predestined for my life and let Your Kingdom rule be established in me. Thank you that no weapon that is formed against me will be able to prosper.

In Jesus' Name I Pray
Amen

ℰ REFLECTIONS ℰ

❧ REFLECTIONS ❧

CHAPTER 6

Conquering Fear
Part 2: What's Love Got to do With It???

Growing in God's Love

I'm sure, you may be asking the question; well what does love have to do with fear? To answer the question let's go to the Word of God.

[7] "Dear friends let us love one another, for love comes from God. Everyone who loves has been born of God and knows God. [8] Whoever does not love does not know God, because God is love. [9] This is how God showed his love among us: He sent his one and only Son into the world that we might live through him. [10] This is love: not that we loved God, but that he loved us and sent his Son as an atoning sacrifice for our sins. [11] Dear friends, since God so loved us, we also ought to love one another. [12] No one has ever seen God; but if we love one another, God lives in us and his love is made complete in us. [13] This is how we know that we live in him and he in us: He has given us of his Spirit. [14] And we have seen and testify that the Father has sent his Son to be the Savior of the world. [15] If anyone acknowledges that Jesus is the Son of God, God lives in them and they in God. [16] And so we know and rely on the love God has for us. God is love. Whoever lives in love lives in God, and God in them. [17] This is how love is made complete among us so that we will have confidence on the day of judgment: In this world we are like Jesus. [18] There is no fear in love."

"But perfect love drives out fear, because fear has to do with punishment. The one who fears is not made perfect in love."

1 John 4:7-18 (NIV)

In this passage of scripture, God deals very candidly with the heart of man about the topic of love. To gain greater understanding, let us break these scriptures down and examine them more closely.

[7] "Dear friends let us love one another for love comes from God. Everyone who loves has been born of God and knows God. [8] Whoever does not love does not know God, because God is love. [9] This is how God showed his love among us: He sent his one and only Son into the world that we might live through him. [10] This is love: not that we loved God, but that he loved us and sent his Son as an atoning sacrifice for our sins. [11] Dear friends, since God so loved us, we also ought to love one another. [12] No one has ever seen God; but if we love one another, God lives in us and his love is made complete in us."

1 John 4:7-12 (NIV)

First of all, we are commanded to love one another. We are then told that love comes from or originates with God. Next, we are told that everyone who operates in love has been born of God and knows God; in contrast, those who do not operate in love do not truly know God. The writer explains that God demonstrated His love toward us (mankind) by sending His only son into the world to be our atoning sacrifice…that is to cover our sins. We are once again admonished to love one another and reassured of God's presence and His love being made complete in us.

[13] "This is how we know that we live in him and He in us: He has given us of his Spirit. [14] And we have seen and testify that the Father has sent his Son to be the Savior of the world. [15] If anyone acknowledges that Jesus is the Son of God, God lives in them and they in God. [16] And so we know and rely on the love God has for us. God is love. Whoever lives in love lives in God, and God in them. [17] This is how love is made complete among us so that we will have confidence on the day of judgment: In this world we are like Jesus. [18] There is no fear in love. But perfect love drives out fear, because fear has to do with punishment. The one who fears is not made perfect in love."

1 John 4:13-18 (NIV)

We have full assurance of God's presence in our lives through the Holy Spirit whom He has given to dwell in us. As children of God, we acknowledge that Jesus, the Son of God, was sent to be the Savior of the world. And because God gave His son for our redemption we can come to know and fully rely on God's immeasurable love for us.

God is the quintessence of love. It is His nature…one of His most distinctive attributes. As we live or abide in God, we bid Him to habitually dwell in us; we dwell in Him and He in us. And as we spend time in His presence God breathes His love into us, inevitably we take on His nature and begin to exhibit His characteristics. This is how God's love is made complete in us. Now verse 18 is the crux of what I want to get to:

18 "There is no fear in love. But perfect love drives out fear, because fear has to do with punishment. The one who fears is not made perfect in love."

1 John 4:18 (NIV)

The Bible says perfect love drives out fear, and the one who fears is not made perfect in love. This simply means that perfect love causes fear to take flight. Fear has to do with punishment, and God would not have His children living under condemnation and fear of penalty when He has already redeemed us through the precious blood of His Son. The spirit of fear and pure God-breathed love cannot co-habitat in the life of a believer. They cannot coexist. One will dominate and drive the other out. When the love of

God is truly perfected or made complete in us, fear has no place…it is forced to leave.

You may be asking yourself, how can I be made complete in the love of God? By abiding in His Word, spending time in His presence, and living in faithful obedience to Him. It is vital to understand that we cannot and will not grow to maturity in God's love without spending time in His presence and in His Word. The more time we spend with Him, the more we grow to love Him. And the more our love for Him intensifies, the more our love will become evident to those with whom we come in contact. God's desire is that we be filled with boldness which comes with confidence in knowing and abiding in Him. It is His will that we come to experience a true breakthrough.

The Breakthrough

I would like to take a moment to define *BREAKTHROUGH*

The word breakthrough is derived of two words (Break & Through) making it a compound word. To begin let's look at the definition of these words individually.

BREAK:
1. To separate into parts with violence or suddenness.
2. To collapse or give way.

3. To change suddenly.
4. To destroy the continuity of.
5. To demolish
6. To shatter
7. To smash
8. To rupture or burst
9. To interrupt

An examination of the word *through* yields the following definitions:

THROUGH

1. From the beginning to the end.
2. Completely across or over.
3. In one side and out the other.
4. Between or among the parts of.
5. All the way to completion.

When both words are placed together, ***BREAKTHROUGH*** can be defined as:

1. A penetration as by military forces. (See Ephesians 6:11-18).
2. To collapse or give way between or among the parts of.

Thus, a breakthrough is an action which has or is taking place in the realm of the spirit, by which the continuity of a stronghold in your life has been interrupted as a result of penetration from the Word of God. The Word of God causes a rupture, leaving an opening through which you are able to burst, shatter, and ultimately destroy its' power in your life. Once this action is completed in the spirit it then crosses over into the natural realm where it causes a sudden change to manifest in your life. The atmosphere shifts, healing, deliverance, and restoration take place. You are renewed, refined, empowered, and elevated. What was once a stronghold is destroyed all the way to completion, it is demolished from one side (the spirit realm) to another (the natural realm). You now begin to live in the manifestation of your prayers. This is your season of breakthrough, walk confidently knowing that God has empowered and equipped you for the journey. The victory is already yours.

PRAYER

Father, as I war against the spirit of fear, I realize that the battle is not mine, but it belongs to you. I declare Your Word over my life, and thank you that you have already sent your angels before me to establish every Word spoken according to Your will. Show me the steps You would have me to take and as I move in faith, I ask You to stir up the Holy Spirit in me. Father Your Word tells me to give no place to the devil, therefore I ask You to remove everything in me that is not of You and fill me with Your love. Fill me until I overflow. I confess my need for You to permeate every area of my life with Your love. Perfect me in Your love and Your love in me so that I may walk in total confidence of complete deliverance from fear. As I walk out my deliverance, I thank you that you are with me and in me, continually empowering me to overcome the stronghold of fear. Father I open myself to you yielding to the guidance of your Holy Spirit. I receive your deliverance, knowing that when you save, heal and deliver, you do it to the utmost I thank you for watching over Your Word to perform it in my life.

In Jesus' Name I Pray
Amen

❧ REFLECTIONS ❧

◌ঽ REFLECTIONS ◌ঽ

CHAPTER 7

Maintaining Your Deliverance

You have reached an important milestone in your journey towards freedom. As you continue to walk out your deliverance, please allow me to give you a word of warning. You will experience some resistance. The enemy will try to fight you by using various intimidation tactics. He will proceed strategically by launching attacks against your mind and attempting to whisper lies to you. Some of his tactics will include attacking your self-esteem, for example, (you are not good enough, no one will benefit from it, you can't do it, it's not going to work, and you don't have the resources). These are all lies the enemy uses in an attempt to hinder us from receiving our deliverance and walking in divine purpose. Be careful who you allow to speak into your life as the enemy will often employ people who are closest to you to plant negative seeds. Press through the opposition because your breakthrough is on the other side of your ability to persevere.

❖ Submerge yourself in the Word of God. Quote the Word over your life, meditate on it, allow your mind to be renewed and transform the way you react to the enemy's fear tactics. It is God's Word that will sustain you and keep you in the knowledge of Truth.

❖ Don't fret, because as a child of God you already have the victory over and against the attacks of the enemy.

❖ Don't give up, because the God of the universe has your back. He understands and is working in you to perfect His will for your life.

❖ Don't back down, press your way through it using a combination of God's Word, prayer, and acts of faith.

❖ Always keep your spiritual antennas up by asking and allowing the Holy Spirit to expose the enemy's plans, and then attack them with the Word of God.

❖ Don't stop, be persistent…as you continue to implement these principles in your life you will experience a true breakthrough.

I would now like to take a moment and pray over you. Let us touch and agree.

My Prayer for You

Heavenly Father, in the name of your son Jesus, I boldly approach the throne of grace acknowledging You as the Alpha and the Omega; You are the one true God, the all sufficient, Holy One. Thank you for the abundant grace you shower down upon us with each new day. Father I confess my confidence in Your ability to do exceeding abundantly above all I may ask or even think according to Your power which is at work in me.

Father, your Word says, "The prayers of the righteous avail much" I come interceding on behalf of my brother/sister, pleading the blood of Jesus over and around him/her. I come against the spirit of fear and decree that **no weapon** formed against my brother/sister shall prosper. I ask you to form a hedge of protection around him/her and I decree that no perforation or penetration exists in that hedge; I seal it in the name of Jesus and by the power of the Holy Spirit.

Father You have given me the keys to the Kingdom of Heaven; therefore, I bind the spirit of fear and curse it at the root. I command it to cease in its' attacks now. I denounce **every** lying and false spirit associated with the spirit of fear. I declare that these spirits are now released from their assignments in my brother/sister's life. And I decree that every stronghold and generational curse associated with the spirit of fear is now broken.

Let every plot, plan, and tactic of the enemy fail and be returned double-fold to the one who sent them. And I command every spirit that has been released from their assignment to go forth now and become part of Jesus' footstool. I seal them there by the blood, in the name of Jesus, and by the power of the Holy Spirit. Release upon my brother/sister a new sense of purpose and a fresh anointing. I declare that my brother/sister is now free to walk in Your divinely appointed destiny for his/her life. Cause him/her to go forth in boldness and power.

In Jesus' Name I Pray
Amen

As you continue to exercise the strategies and principles in this book, you will come to experience a new level of freedom in your pursuit of God's plan for your life. Remain focused on your mission and remember…**The Victory is Already Yours!**

❧ REFLECTIONS ❧

⊗ REFLECTIONS ⊗

☙ Closing Prayer ☙

Dear Reader,

Thank you for reading *The Power to Overcome Fear: Breaking Free From the Enemies Grip!* My Prayer is that you have been sensitive to the Spirit **_of_** God and that you have received a Word **_from_** God. I hope you have been empowered and enlightened by the content of this book.

May God continue to bless and guide you as you fearlessly pursue His divine purpose for your life.

Thedoshia

ଔ Scriptural Helps ଔ

II Timothy 1:7
For God hath not given us the spirit of fear; but of power, and of love, and of a sound mind.

Romans 8:15
For ye have not received the spirit of bondage again to fear; but ye have received the Spirit of adoption, whereby we cry Abba, Father.

I John 4:18
There is no fear in love; but perfect love casteth out fear: because fear hath torment. He that feareth is not made perfect in love.

Psalm 91
[1]He that dwelleth in the secret place of the most High shall abide under the shadow of the Almighty. [2]I will say of the Lord, He is my refuge and my fortress: my God in Him will I trust.[3]Surely He shall deliver thee from the snare of the fowler, and from the noisome pestilence.[4]He shall cover thee with his feathers, and under his wings shalt thou trust: his truth shall be thy shield and buckler.[5]Thou shalt not be afraid for the terror by night; nor for the arrow that flieth by day.[6]Nor for the pestilence that walketh in darkness; nor for the destruction that wasteth at noonday.[7]A thousand shall fall at thy side, and ten thousand at thy right hand; but it shall not come nigh thee.[8]Only with thine eyes shalt thou behold and see the reward of the wicked.[9]Because thou hast made the Lord, which is my refuge, even the most High, thy habitation;[10]There shall no evil befall thee, neither shall

any plague come nigh thy dwelling.[11]For he shall give his angels charge over thee, to keep thee in all thy ways.[12]They shall bear thee up in their hands, lest thou dash thou foot against a stone.[13]Thou shalt tread upon the lion and the adder: the young lion and the dragon shalt thou trample under feet.[14]Because he hath set his love upon me, therefore will I deliver him: I will set him on high, because he hath known my name. [15]He shall call upon me, and I will answer him: I will be with him in trouble; I will deliver him, and honour him.[16]With long life will I satisfy him, and show him my salvation.

Proverbs 3:25-26
Be not afraid of sudden fear, neither of the desolation of the wicked, when it cometh. For the Lord shall be thy confidence, and shall keep thy foot from being taken.

Isaiah 54:14
In righteousness shalt thou be established; thou shalt be far from oppression; thou shalt not fear; and from terror; for it shall not come near thee.

Psalm 56:11
In God have I put my trust: I will not be afraid what man can do unto me.

Psalm 23
[1]The Lord is my shepherd; I shall not want.[2] He maketh me to lie down in green pastures; he leadeth me beside the still waters.[3]He restoreth my soul: he leadeth me in the paths of righteousness for his name sake.[4]Yea, though I walk through the valley of the shadow of death, I will fear no evil: for thou art with me; thy rod and thy staff they

comfort me.⁵Thou prepares a table before me in the presence of mine enemies: thou anointest my head with oil; my cup runneth over.⁶Surely goodness and mercy shall follow me all the days of my life: and I will dwell in the house of the Lord for ever.

Psalm 31:24

Be of good courage, and he shall strengthen your heart, all ye that hope in the Lord.

John 14:27

Peace I leave with you, my peace I give unto you: not as the world giveth, give I unto you. Let not your heart be troubled, neither let it be afraid.

Psalm 27

[1]The Lord is my light and my salvation; whom shall I fear? The Lord is the strength of my life; of whom shall I be afraid? [2] When the wicked, even mine enemies and foes, came upon me to eat up my flesh, they stumbled and fell.[3]Though an host should encamp against me, my heart shall not fear: though war should rise against me, in will I be confident.[4]One thing have I desired of the Lord, that will I seek after; that I may dwell in the house of the Lord all the days of my life, to behold the beauty of the Lord, and to enquire in his temple.[5]For in the time of trouble he shall hide me in his pavilion: in the secret of his tabernacle shall he hide me; he shall set me up upon a rock.[6]And now shall mine head be lifted up above mine enemies round about me: therefore will I offer in his tabernacle sacrifices of joy; I will sing, yea, I will sing praises unto the Lord.

Hebrews 13:6

So that we may boldly say, The Lord is my helper, and I will not fear what man shall do unto me.

Isaiah 41:10, 13-14

[10] Fear not, for I am with you; Be not dismayed, for I am your God. I will strengthen you, Yes I will help you, I will uphold you with my righteous right hand. [13]For I, the Lord your God, will hold your right hand, Saying to you, "Fear not, I will help you. [14]"Fear not, you worm Jacob, You men of Israel! I will help you," says the LORD and your Redeemer, the Holy One of Israel.

Isaiah 43:1

But now, thus says the Lord, who created you' O Jacob, And He who formed you O Israel: "Fear not, for I have redeemed you; I have called you by your name; You are mine."

Isaiah 44:8

"Do not fear, nor be afraid; Have I not told you from that time, and declared it? You are my witnesses. Is there a God besides me? Indeed, there is no other Rock; I know not one"

Isaiah 51:7

"Listen to Me, you who know righteousness, You people in whose heart fear my law: Do not fear the reproach of men, Nor be afraid of their insults."

Joel 2:21
Fear not, O land; Be glad and rejoice, For the Lord has done marvelous things!

Haggai 2:5
"According to the word that I covenanted with you when you came out of Egypt, so My Spirit remains among you; do not fear!"

Matthew 10:28
And do not fear those who can kill the body but cannot kill the soul. But rather fear Him who is able to destroy both soul and body in hell.

Matthew 10:31
Do not fear therefore; You are of more value than many sparrows.

Luke 12:4
"And I say to you my friends; do not be afraid of those who kill the body, and after that have no more that they can do."

Luke 12:7
But the very hairs of your head are numbered. Do not fear therefore; you are of more value than many sparrows."

Luke 12:32
"Do not fear, little flock, for it is your Father's good pleasure to give you the kingdom."

Joshua 1:9

Have I not commanded you? Be strong and of good courage; do not be afraid, nor be dismayed, for the Lord your God is with you wherever you go.

Genesis 26:24

I am the God of your father Abraham; do not fear, for I am with you.

Numbers 21:34

Do not fear him, for I have delivered him [your enemy] into your hand.

Deuteronomy 1:21

Look, the LORD your God has set the land before you; go up and possess it, as the LORD God of your fathers has spoken to you; do not fear or be discouraged.

Deuteronomy 3:22

You must not fear them [spiritual or natural enemies], for the LORD your God himself fights for you.

Deuteronomy 31:6, 8

6"Be strong and of good courage, do not fear nor be afraid of them; for the Lord your God, He is the One who goes with you. He will not leave you nor forsake you."

8 "And the LORD, He is the One who goes before you. He will be with you; He will not leave you nor forsake you; do not fear nor be dismayed."

I Chronicles 28:20
And David said to his son Solomon, "Be strong and of good courage, and do it; do not fear nor be dismayed, for the Lord God, my God, will be with you. He will not leave you nor forsake you, until you have finished all the work for the service of the house of the LORD."

Psalm 37:4
The Angel of the Lord encamps all around those who fear Him, and delivers them.

Psalm 56:4
In God I will praise his word, in God I have put my trust; I will not fear what flesh can do unto me.

Psalm 118:6
The Lord is on my side; I will not fear; what can man do unto me?

᧐ᔆ Invitation ᧐ᔆ

If you were to die today, where you would spend eternity? The Bible says,

⁹That if you confess with your mouth, "Jesus is Lord" and believe in your heart that God raised him from the dead, you will be saved. ¹⁰For it is with your heart that you believe and are justified, and it is with your mouth that you confess and are saved."

Romans 10:9-10 (NIV)

It is not God's will for any man to perish but for all to come to a place of repentance. He loves us so much that even while we were still sinners, He gave his only son Jesus to die for our sins so that we, through him, might have eternal life. If you would like to secure your place in heaven, pray this prayer with me.

God, I confess that I am a sinner. I believe that Jesus is your Son, that He died for my sins and that You raised Him from the dead. I confess my need for You, and ask You now to come into my heart and save me. I receive Jesus as my Savior and I will make Him my Lord.

In Jesus' Name I Pray
Amen

Signed:_____

Date:_____

❧ REFLECTIONS ❧

❧ REFLECTIONS ❧

❧ REFLECTIONS ❧